Stane Street
From Chichester to London

Richard Powell

Published in 2021 by

U P Publications, St George's House, George St,
Huntingdon, Cambridgeshire, PE29 3GH. UK
+44 208 133 0123 manager@uppublications.ltd.uk

© 2021 Richard Powell

Richard Powell has asserted his moral rights
under the Copyright, Designs & Patents Act 1988,
to be identified as the Author of this Work

All Rights Reserved - No part of this publication may be
reproduced or transmitted by any means, electronic,
mechanical, photocopy or otherwise, without the prior
permission of the author or publisher except for the
purpose of research or editorial use. This is a work of
non-fiction based on the information available at the
time of publication and the author's experience in the field.
Image credits and copyrights are listed at the back of the
book. A catalogue record for this book is available from the
British Library. Licensed Fonts: Caviar Dreams, Concept.

ISBN 13: 978-1-912777-31-0

www.uppbooks.com

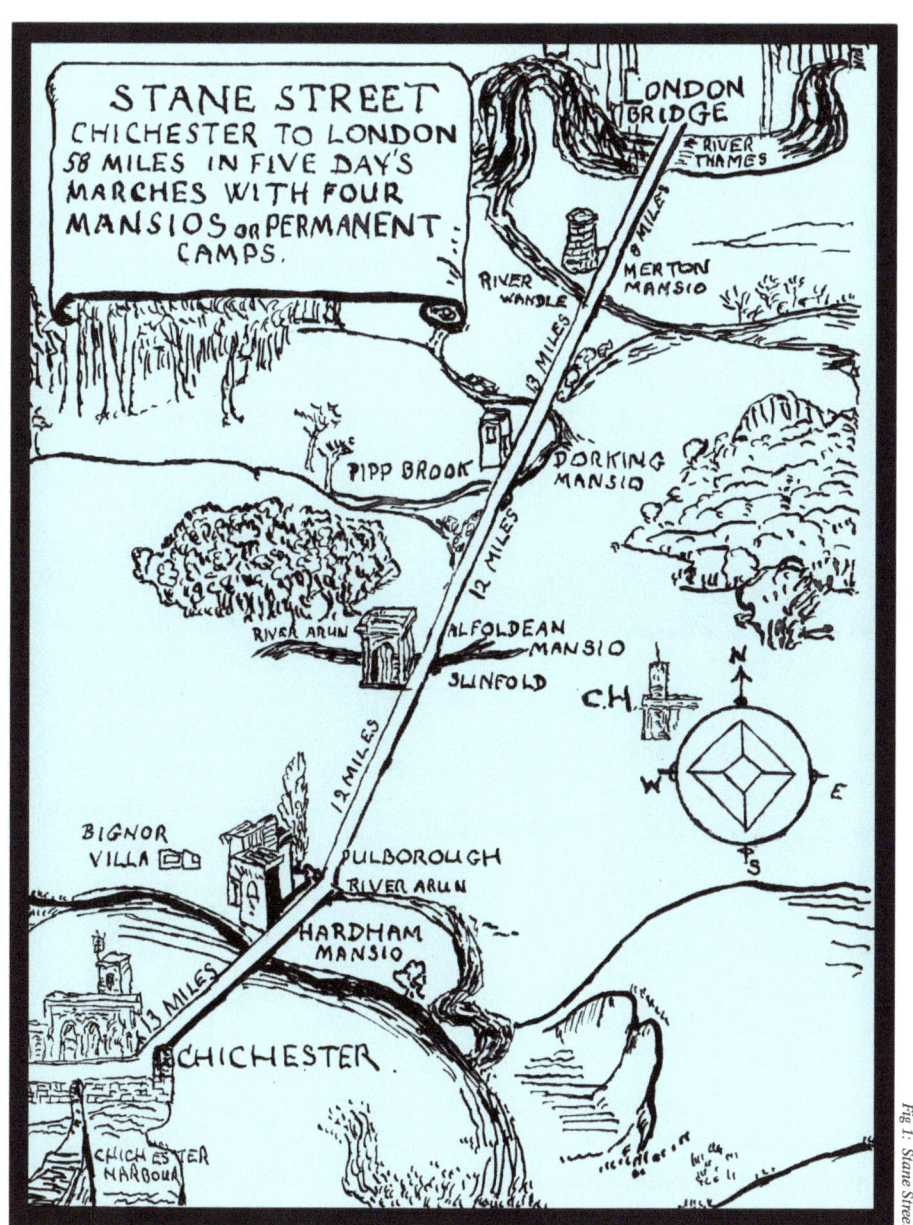

Fig 1: Stane Street

Introduction
by Richard Powell

Fig 2: Julius Caesar Peter Paul Rubens

This book contains stories and pictures of the people and places along the 58 mile, 2,000-year-old road we know as Stane Street, from the time before the Romans to the current era.

In 55 BC Julius Caesar led the first invasion of England. He did not get very far and left the next year.

For the following 98 years the people of Britain traded with the Romans and paid tributes to Rome, to avoid another invasion. In 43AD, Emperor Claudius sent General Aulus Plautius with four legions to conquer England. Historians cannot quite agree but think they sailed from Boulogne to Noviomagus, present day Chichester. Over the next 30 years they managed to conquer what is now England, Wales and part of Scotland.

In 383AD Rome began the withdrawal of troops for use on other frontiers of the empire. Having stripped British Garrisons in 406AD, Rome's weak presence in Britain was highlighted in 410AD when the Romano-British settlements ejected the last Rome-appointed Magisters, unopposed, as Rome's troops were needed in other areas of the empire to fight barbarian incursions closer to Rome. This left the tribes of Britain on their own to fight the Anglo-Saxon invaders.

One of the things the Romans left was a network of roads, not equalled again until the 18th Century with the advent of the turnpike toll roads.

Roman roads were paved, well-engineered and usually fairly straight, as they needed to move troops and equipment quickly.

Fig 3: Road Construction

As time progressed, they became a tool of commerce providing easy transport for trade goods with way stations and administrations centres.

One of the first roads to be built after the original Roman invasion was the road from Noviomagus to the bridge at Londinium.

Much of the invading army and equipment arrived at the harbour at Chichester and was needed in London to carry on the campaign.

Noviomagus quickly became a flourishing walled city with villas, markets, baths, a forum and an amphitheatre.

The road to Londinium was built within ten years of the initial invasion.

Traffic was heavy, with four army forts built along the way for protection and a place to stay.

Soon villages were established along the route and commerce flourished, dramatically changing the lives of local tribes.

From Iron Age hill fort dwellers to farmers, shepherds, tradesmen and merchants, the road changed the economics and culture of the region in such a profound way its influence can still be felt.

Enjoy the ride, follow the route and I hope you will find a few stories of your own along the way.

High Tech or Line of Sight?

Fig 4: Hilaire Belloc c.1903

There is some controversy about the how the Romans actually created such a straight road. Hilaire Belloc, one of the most prolific English writers of the early 20th century lived at Slindon which is very close to Stane Street.

He is well known for his great love of England and especially Sussex. He wrote travel books, poetry, politics, children's stories and much more.

The West Sussex Library produced a pamphlet in 2000 giving a biography and information about Belloc's writing called The Path to Rome. In 1913 he published a book called The Stane Street in which he describes in detail the route and layout of this old Roman stone road. He was fascinated by how straight the Romans could build it. Actually, it is not quite straight, but is made up of extremely long straight stretches built point to point. He questioned how the Romans could do this.

Was it just line of sight or did they have a sophisticated technology more advanced than we know?

One of the problems with the 'line of sight' arguments, is that they needed outstanding features, such as hills, to follow a sight line over a distance. Both Chichester and London are near sea level so there is nothing high enough to use as a sighting point. How did they choose which direction to head for when they started? They had only been in the country a few years.

In 1923 Capt. W. A. Grant published his book The Topography of Stane Street purporting that the Romans had some technology which gave them a straight-line direction between the two centres. This created some heated arguments in letters to the editor of different publications by learned academics of the time. They claimed that the road had to be line of sight. One even suggested that the roads were there before the Romans came.

In Pre-Roman time the iron age tribes of Sussex had taken to living and fortifying the tops of hills. The quickest way to get from one to the other would be a straight road, i.e. line of sight, so all the Romans did was pave them. The jury is still out on this one. Does it really matter? What we do know is that the Romans paved them and traces are still here nearly 2,000 years later.

The definitive book, *With a Spade on Stane Street*, was published in 1936 by classics historian and archaeologist S. E. Winbolt. He describes every foot of the road from end to end, often correcting Belloc. Both the book by Belloc and Winbolt's rebuttal have helped me greatly in putting together this book as they describe features that have disappeared over the years. My gratitude to both men.

Fig 5: Bluebells

Fig 6: Chichester Market Cross

Chapter One
Chichester to Goodwood

Starting from the south, Mile Zero is at the east gate to the Roman walled town of Noviomagus Reginorum. This was the name used by the Romans for what is now the present-day city of Chichester. The road heads northeast from here toward the capital of Roman Britain, Londinium.

Noviomagus means 'new fields'. The Reginorum was added in order to distinguish it from other places named Noviomagus.

Originally established as a fort, it quickly changed into a Roman-British town. The locals were friendly and the town prospered. It soon boasted an amphitheatre, baths, temples, markets and industries. It's well worth the time to visit the remains of the Roman Villa at Fishbourne, just west of Chichester. Besides the mosaics there are parts of the structure and the first garden in Britain. The Romans may have been some of the first Christians in Sussex as the chi-rho motif was found near Wiggonholt, a few miles along Stane Street near Pulborough. Because of the Saxon raids the town was abandoned by the end of the 4th century.

Eventually it was captured by the Saxons and named after Cissa (Chichester).

Many of the ruins were reused in the new town. Look carefully and you can find Roman stones in some of the old walls.

Fig 7: Romans Ancient Times

Fig 8: Chi-rho Motif

Christianity came to this area again in 681 with St. Wilfred who set up a church in Selsey just south of Chichester.

With the Normans, in 1075, the seat of the church was moved to Chichester Cathedral. The cathedral has a remarkably interesting history and should be toured to appreciate its 900 years of existence. Other things of interest are the Market Cross, built in 1501 at the intersection of the four main streets in the city centre, and many historical buildings. The city has a symphony orchestra and a football club. It also hosts a month-long music festival, the famous Chichester Festival Theatre, and a fair that started 800 years ago and is held every October: a must see for any visitor to southern England. Oddly, at the actual beginning of Stane Street in Chichester is a popular Italian restaurant and delicatessen. The Romans could not just stay away.

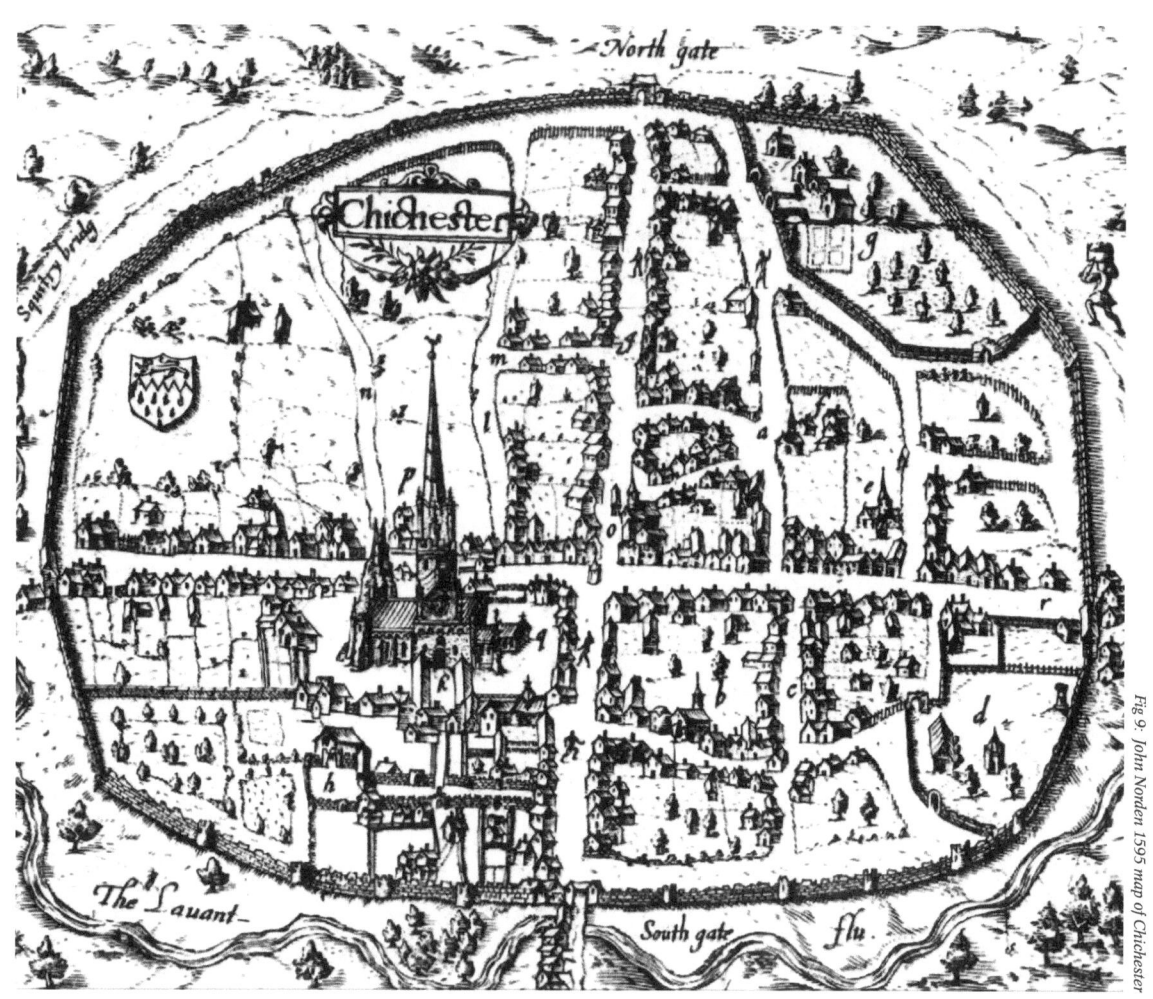

Fig 9: John Norden 1595 map of Chichester

Fig 10: St Pancras Church

Mile Zero is where the medieval church of St. Pancras was built around year 1100. It was destroyed during the civil war and rebuilt in 1749/50. The Victorians remodelled it in the 19th century and more changes were made in the 20th century. It is still very active today. Looking up Stane Street, which here is called St. Pancras Road or the A286, we can see how straight it is. The first 100 meters is commercial, with ethnic restaurants, a pub and some shops. This will bring us up to Litten Garden and the Chichester War memorial.

If we veer off Stane Street here to the left and follow the A286 for 50 meters, we pass the Chichester Cinema and come upon Priory Park on the left. The old Roman walls, found here, had fallen into disrepair until the Victorians thought up a good use for them. They planted trees and made a lovely promenade

Fig 11: Roman Wall

Fig 12: Litten Park

around the city. Beyond the park can be found the University and St. Richard's Hospital.

Back now to Stane Street and Litten Gardens where the city keeps the park and the cenotaph in beautiful condition. Held here every year, Memorial parades commemorate the sacrifice of the Chichester men and women in defence of their country. Behind the Memorial is the playing field for the Chichester Sharks American Football Club.

Here the A286 becomes the A285, and traffic is no longer just one way. The road continues past a mixture of commercial properties, residential housing and a school. At the next roundabout, the name changes from St. Pancras to Westhampnett Road. Continue to the big roundabout and bear left staying on Westhampnett Road. Following the line of sight, which would have been the Roman Road, we come to Mile 1 in the middle of the superstore parking lot. Continuing to follow this line would get very wet as it crosses the north west corner of a large reservoir.

Around this spot, in the 18th and 19th centuries (where the shopping mall now sits), was a turnpike toll booth. With the advent of more middle classes and wealthy merchants the need for well-maintained roads increased.

An act of parliament created 'Turnpike Trusts' which charged tolls in exchange for the upkeep of the road.

The toll booth usually consisted of a house for the keeper and his family. At its peak, in the early 1800s, there were almost 8,000 toll gates active in England. Trains put most out of business by the end of the Victorian period. In 1888 the government made road maintenance the responsibility of the county councils.

The road crosses a small roundabout and then a large one at the Chichester by-pass.

This puts us on a road marked as Stane Street and on to the village of Westhampnettt. Rolls Royce has an assembly plant just north of here built on the Goodwood Estate in 2003. During WWII, Rolls Royce engines powered Spitfires, Hurricanes, bombers and even the American P-51 Mustangs.

During the Battle of Britain in 1940, RAF Westhampnett was built as fighter base, first for British Spitfires and later for American fighter planes.

Fig 13: Spitfire Formation by Gareth Davies Rolls Royce Engines

There has been a church here since the 8th century. We can see that some of the material in the walls was taken from the Roman road. Additions were made to the Saxon church in the 13th century and the Victorians added their bit in the 1800s. It was on the pilgrim way from Winchester to Salisbury through St. Richard's in Chichester. The pilgrims inscribed waymarks in the chancel. The present church of St. Peter is a Grade II listed building.

The graveyard is worth a visit, as three bishops of Chichester are buried there, plus James Lillywhite, captain of the English Cricket team that played the first ever test match in Australia in 1877.

Fig 14: James Lillywhite 1860s

Diverting to the southeast, we come upon the ancient village of Tangmere. There are records going back to the 7th century when the Saxon king gave the area to St. Wilfred, then the bishop of York. The church of St. Andrew was built on a Saxon wooden church site that was probably built over a pagan site. Here too some of the material in the walls come from the Roman Road and the abandoned city of Noviomagus. It has one of the oldest Yew trees in England at its present front door.

RAF Tangmere has been used since 1917 (originally by the Royal Flying Corp).

During WWII it was one of the most important fighter bases, getting its first Spitfire squadron in 1940. It was crucial for the protection of the south coast. during the Battle of Britain.

The airfield was badly bombed, and planes destroyed on the ground, but was operational again within 5 days.

The SOE (Special Operations Executive) used it as a supply and drop-off centre for the resistance in occupied Europe. The Tangmere Military Aviation Museum provides an excellent day out.

Turning west at New Road takes us to Goodwood in about a kilometre. The estate has been the seat of the Dukes of Richmond since 1697. Here we find an airfield in the middle of a motor racecourse track.

Fig 15: Goodwood Vintage Auto Race – Courtesy of Goodwood Estate

Farther on we come across the manor house, hotel, golf course and horse racing course.

Goodwood is the host to many spectacular events throughout the year, notably the Festival of Speed (car racing), Goodwood Revival (classic cars), and Glorious Goodwood (horse racing).

Their website has all the activities in detail.

Turning south at The Street we continue to the village of Boxgrove. In 1982, flint tools and a hominin tibia were discovered in a gravel quarry at Boxgrove.

These were dated back over 500,000 years and are recognised to be the earliest evidence of human occupation in Britain.

Here also are the ruins of the Boxgrove Priory, a Benedictine monastery built around 1100AD and destroyed in the 16th century with Henry VIII's Dissolution of the Monasteries.

The parish church has also been destroyed but the abbey church remains. It is much larger than would be expected for such a small village - a spectacular church still active today. Both the ruins and the church are well worth a visit.

Fig 16: Boxgrove Priory and Church

Just past the village of Halnaker, the A285 curves around Halnaker Hill which is the highest spot around there. Stane Street continues across the shoulder of the hill, but it appears that locals found it easier to go around.

If we follow the Roman road, we will also notice that for the first half mile it seems to have sunk over a metre and become a tunnel with overlapping tree branches.

The reason is probably because this road was used for centuries to get grain up and flour down from the windmill at the top of Halnaker Hill.

Fig 17: Road up Halnaker Hill

The road to the mill turns off to the west about a half a kilometre from where the highway curves and the old Mill Cottage can be found.

History books tell us the present mill was built in 1740 to replace the one built in 1540.

That would account for a lot of horses and wagons going over that part of the road.

The windmill was badly damaged in the early 20th century by lightning and storms.

It was restored to its former glory in the summer of 1934.

The sails were replaced in the summer of 2016.

Being the highest hill around these parts it was used as an observation post during WWII. There are some remains of these activities near the windmill.

The road drops down, passing through fields of grain and corn, old farms and small copses of oak and beech.

Fig 18: Halnaker Windmill

Fig 19: Vineyard

Wildflowers and lovely views of the downs on all sides make this part of the route very memorable.

At the bottom of the slope the A285 appears again, following the original road.

Fig 20: Wildflowers

Fig 21: Stane Street near Eartham

Chapter Two
Bignor Hill

The next five miles of the street travels through woodland, grazing fields, and farms. This section is through the South Downs National Park, which is England's newest national park; created in April 2010. It runs up and over Bignor Hill, then downward towards the village of Bignor and the remains of a Roman Villa.

The road leaves the A285, which curves west, and north on to Petworth. a worthwhile side trip. Petworth is a lovely medieval market town in the South Downs. In September 1942, the Germans bombed the town, destroying the Petworth Boys School and killing over 30 people, mostly students and teachers. The target was believed to be Petworth House. Petworth House and Park contain the finest collection of artwork owned by the National Trust.

Back to Stane Street, which follows a wooded trail past several

Fig 22: Great Ballard School

fields until reaching a road leading to the village of Eartham, about 1/2 km south. Eartham has a couple of noteworthy points of interest not to be missed.

Great Ballard School is a co-educational independent school for children from 2 1/2 to 13. It was established in 1920 and been located here since 1961.

The school is in Eartham House, built in 1800. The man who owned it, William Huskisson was the first man in the world to be killed by a train. In 1830 he was run over by the "Rocket" during the opening of a railway from Liverpool to Manchester.

The parish church of St. Margaret is over 900 years old, built of flint with many fascinating features. Restored in 1869, it has Queen Victoria's coat of arms in tiles on the chancel floor.

There is centuries-old graffiti on one of the columns. You can also find memorials to artists and politicians including Huskisson.

Stane Street now follows its natural course through Eartham Wood along a bridle path on the Monarch's Way trail.

The Monarch's way is over 600 miles long and is reputed to be the escape route of Charles II in 1651.

The wood is controlled by the Forestry Commission of England, part of the Woodland Trust.

After following the Monarch's Way for about a mile we come out of the forest at 6 corners.

There are now actually 8 corners there, where different trails all cross at the same place.

One of the pathways leading off from here is called Leper's Walk.

This may have been part of a pilgrim's way leading to Canterbury Cathedral.

Stane Street continues past the crossroads and heads up Bignor Hill.

The trail passes through a narrow strip of woods between farmed fields.

The path is overhung by these trees and massive roots appear along the way.

The roots do not appear to be able to get through the old Roman road.

The trees soon disappear, and open fields are on both sides.

About a half mile from the 6 corners, there is a large farmhouse and outbuildings on the south side of the path.

Fig 23: Six Corners

Fig 24: Tree Roots over road

This is Gumber Bothy.

A bothy is a place that supplies basic accommodation like a hostel.

This one is on the National Trust's Slindon Estate.

It is a converted flint barn on a working sheep farm.

It is open from March to October for walkers, cyclists and horse riders, (no cars) staying either in dorms or camping. Basic kitchen and bathroom facilities are supplied.

Sightings of deer, badgers and the Gumber swallows are included in the price.

Fig 25: Gumber Bothy

At the top of the field above the farm are traces of Iron Age farming.

In April, the forest floors are covered with bluebells and the nearby Slindon estate is worth a stop to take some very striking pictures.

The next half mile of the road is a steady climb toward the top of the hill.

Open pasture is on both sides of the raised trail. Be careful not to bother the sheep during lambing season.

Fig 26: Stane Streeet Looking South

Fig 27: Stane Streeet at Monarch Way

Onward through light sparse woods and open fields we cross a turnstile and the Monarch's Way meets up with the South Downs Way.

This trail is completely within the South Downs National Park covering over 100 miles from Eastbourne to Winchester.

It passes through some of the most beautiful landscapes and villages in southern England.

This path comes near an Iron Age fort to the south and modern radio towers to the north.

A bit of a contrast.

The road here is raised quite high above the adjacent fields.

At the parking lot at the top of the hill the view looking north over the South Downs is amazing.

Be sure to take a good look at the road sign at the top of the parking lot.

The next mile of the road has disappeared into the trees on the downhill side of the hill.

The access road runs parallel to where it probably was. Nearby is the tiny hamlet of Bignor, one of the quietest corners of West Sussex.

There is no pub, and the closest rail station is 3 1/2 miles away in Amberley.

The only access is by narrow country lanes from the A29 at Bury. It does have a few interesting points worth noting.

The Norman church (Holy Cross) has a quiet beauty, set in a peaceful graveyard.

Fig 28: Signpost on top of Bignor Hill

Fig 29: Wealdon Hall

The Yeoman's house is a 15th century Wealden hall house.

Built around 1420 it has been modernised by the present owners without losing historic features.

During WWII Bignor Manor House was used by British Intelligence as a secret forward base for resistance agents being flown to France from RAF Tangmere, and a debriefing base for those returning.

Just to the east of Bignor and west of the road's path are the remains of a massive 65 room Roman villa built in the 1st century.

The ruins were discovered in 1812 by a farmer ploughing the field.

The site was excavated and opened to the public in 1814.

For over 200 years it has been an extremely popular attraction.

Although not as big or important as the Roman palace found at Fishbourne, near Chichester, this villa has beautifully intact mosaic floors.

Also to be seen, is the central heating using hot air under the tiled floors.

To protect the excavations and

Fig. 30. Roman Mosaics

the floors, the Georgians constructed buildings over the site.

These in themselves have become historically interesting Grade 2 listed buildings.

Across the road from the villa are grape vineyards planted in the last few years.

The villa makes a great day out, combining a drive up Bignor Hill with a walk along Stane Street.

In the narrow country lanes from Bignor to the A29, we pass through West Burton, which contains some memorable old homes.

Viscountess Francis Wolseley in one of her series of articles for Sussex County Magazine in the 1920s and 30s, on the historic houses of Sussex, fondly describes Coke's House in West Burton.

First built in 1557 the house was destroyed by fire and rebuilt in the early 1600s by the Cooke family.

The house and gardens are still there, well maintained, but privately owned and not open to visitors.

Free range eggs and other produce can be purchased at the farm next door.

Fig 31: Coke's Hall

We can peek over the wall at this Elizabethan beauty and its gardens.

Back at the A29, why not visit the quiet village of Bury? The lovely pub at the highway used to be a stop on the turnpike. The road winds down to the Arun River and the ancient church of St. John the Baptist.

Fig 32: Sign at Bury

For many years a ferry ran across the river here. By the church, Dorest House School is one of the oldest English prep schools.

John Galsworthy, the author of the Forsyth Saga spent the last 7 years of his life here at Bury House.

Back at the A29, Bury Road, we go north for a mile and follow the sharp right turn onto Beacon Hill Road which soon changes its name to London Road. Now we head to the flood plains of the River Arun.

Fig 33: Foxglove

Fig 34: St. Giles Church, Coldwaltham

Chapter Three
Bury to Hardham

The next four miles of the road take us from Bignor Villa to the site of a Roman military mansio. A mansio is defined as a stopping place on a Roman Road maintained by the central government for official use.

Most of the road has vanished under ploughed fields or pasture. Here and there we can follow where it was, as it marks boundaries.

After the Romans left, the Downs' farmers left too, as there was no protection from the Saxon raiders.

The farms went unused, and the road slowly disappeared as it was overgrown and undermined.

Later, after the Saxons settled, they superstitiously avoided Roman remains believing they had been built by an ancient tribe of giants and their souls still haunted the ruins. They built their villages in the lowlands, connecting them with their own roads.

In places on these roads, you can see materials scavenged from Stane Street.

Along here the A29 parallels the road slightly to the east.

The theory is that as the road went through wet and marshy ground and was not being maintained, it eventually sank into the soil.

We could probably find parts of it if we dug in the right places. The medieval road followed a path that is higher and drier.

Being very fertile the land has been farmed for centuries. Today we can find some farm shops along this

Fig 35: River Arun

route where we can pick up fresh local produce, meat, eggs and a cup of tea.

The next hamlet's name, Watersfield, may have something to do with the low lands near the Arun River known as water meadows. Between Bury and Watersfield there was a 19th century turnpike toll-gate.

The toll house is long gone but the records show that a forge is still there. Just beyond is the small village of Coldwaltham.

Here we find the 13th century church of St. Giles built on an earlier Saxon church.

An 11th century coffin lid was found in the graveyard and, now resting in the belfry, confirms the earlier church.

The font bowl also dates from Saxon times, but the stand is Victorian.

During this rebuilding in 1870 a lot of exceptionally beautiful stained glass was added.

Some of this was made by Charles Kempe of Kempe Studios, a famous stained glass window designer who studied under William Morris of pre-Raphaelite fame.

Beside the church stands a huge yew tree, one of the oldest in the country, supposedly dated at over 3,000 years.

This indicates that it may have been the site of pagan worship long before Christ was even born.

The locals strongly defend the claim.

Fig. 36: St. Giles Church, Coldwaltham

Fig 37: Yew tree at St. Giles

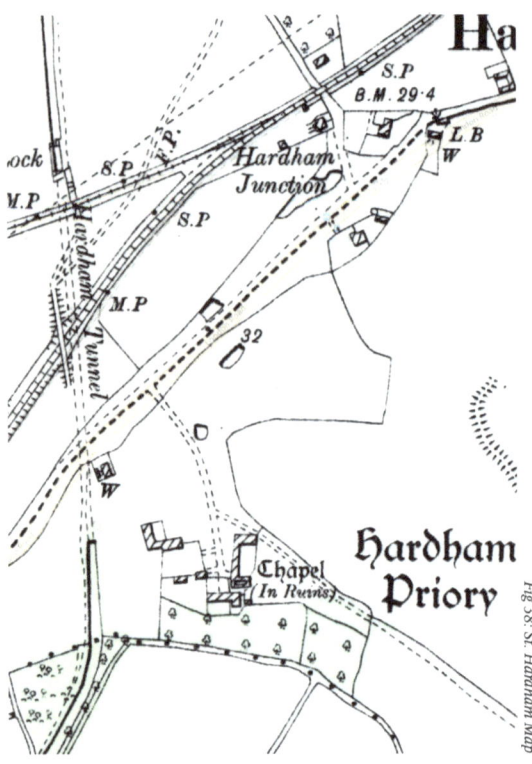

Fig 38: St. Hardham Map

The substantial graveyard extends around 3 sides of the church containing a large section dedicated to victims of WWI.

Nearby is the priest's house, part of which dates to the 13th century. The next hamlet is named Hardham where we find many interesting things to investigate. The village contains some beautifully preserved Elizabethan houses, disused canals and railroads, Roman ruins, and traces of a priory, plus one of the most outstanding little Norman churches in the county. The map shows locations of all these including the abandoned railway that ran through the Roman camp.

An Augustine priory (St. Cross) was built in the 13th century on higher ground overlooking the water lands to the south east. It was abandoned during Henry VIII's reign. The refectory building has been turned into a farmhouse and is a Grade 1 listed building.

Most of the other structures are in ruins. One of the best examples of a house from the Elizabethan period, still occupied, can be found just north of the church. With its low doorways, small windows and timber framed walls, it is hard to imagine the history it has seen over the last 400 years.

Also a Grade I listed building, St.

Fig 39: Elizabethan House

Botolph's, is a simple Norman design church built on the site of an old Saxon church. Building materials (tiles and blocks) from local Roman buildings can be seen used in the walls. The church is best known for its wall paintings (frescoes) believed to have been painted by monks from Lewes, around 1100. They are very well preserved as they were covered with whitewash for centuries and only discovered again during renovations in the 1800s. The pictures include the story of Christ, Adam and Eve and the first known pictures of St. George. One of four, shows him fighting the infidel during the 1st Crusades. Although other Sussex churches have similar paintings, St Botolph is the only one where nearly all the walls are covered. Seeing these is a must.

Fig 40: Frescoes at St. Botolph's

Fig 41: The Wey and Arun Canal

There is a large loop in the Arun River here and a tunnel was built to aid navigation on the Wey & Arun Canal. As with most English canals, they died out as the railways crossed the country in the 19th century.

This canal system connected London with the port at Littlehampton on the South Coast.

The tunnel was closed in 1888 and then filled in by the railway company in 1895.

This was a 'walking' or 'legging' tunnel. Lying on their backs on the top of their vessels and using their feet, the boatmen 'walked' along the roof or walls of the tunnel.

The Midhurst Railway, which used to run from Hardham to Pulborough and points north, opened in 1859 but became a victim of Beecham and closed in the mid-1960s.

The house and gardens at Parham House, just a couple of miles down the road on the A383 are well worth a visit.

When King Henry dissolved the monasteries in 1540, he gave the land, which had belonged to the Monastery of Westminster, to Robert Palmer.

His grandson built the H shaped house in the 1570s. The house was bought and sold many times until, in the 1920s, Clive and Alicia Pearson set about restoring it to its former glory.

The Pearsons and their daughter Veronica Mary Tritton spent more than 60 years restoring Parham,

Fig 42. Parham House

Fig 43: The Long Gallery, Parham House

acquiring items that had originally belonged to the house. The most interesting are in the Long Gallery which is over 160 feet long.

During WWII it was first home to 30 children, evacuees from London. The extensive gardens were covered to grow vegetables, which were shipped off to London. The evacuees were each given an allotment to try on their own. Many developed skills that would never have been learned in London.

Later the mansion was occupied by Canadian officers preparing for the invasion of France.

Fig 44: Parham Gardens

Fig 45: Parham House

The beautiful four acre walled garden, restored, is a big attraction. In the garden is a unique 1920s Wendy House. Not to be missed is the turf and brick maze (not as easy as it looks.) Also on the site is St. Peter's church with its memorials to the Curzin family who occupied Parham House in Victorian times. The views of the South Downs from here are breath-taking. Parham House and garden have been open to the public since 1948.

Another interesting piece of nearby history is the scheduled Historic Monument, the Greatham bridge. This medieval structure first built in 1294, was reconstructed in 1790. Part of it was replaced with a cast iron section, in 1838 after flood damage.

This was the site of a minor battle during the Civil War. It was a strategic point, as it was one of the few places where a bridge crossed the Arun River.

Local Royalists tried to prevent General Waller's army from capturing the bridge. Some of the dead from that clash were hurriedly buried in the village churchyard at Greatham, although their bodies were not discovered until the 1950s when the church vestry collapsed.

It was said to have been used by the future King Charles II on his escape to France.

Set in peaceful countryside on the Arun flood plain, this is a lovely side trip but be careful on the narrow lanes with many blind corners.

Fig 46: Greatham Bridge Detail

Fig 47: Greatham Bridge

Fig. 48: *Morning Glory*

Fig 49: The White Hart Public House at Stopham, near Pulborough

Chapter Four
Over the Arun to Pulborough

The next mile from Hardham and over the bridge to Pulborough is incredibly fascinating. Following the straight line from Coldwaltham we come upon a disused railway.

This railway was closed in the 1960s and all that remains are traces of the bed. Approaching the rail bed, the Roman road turns slightly to the east pointing directly at the old bridge at Pulborough.

Once again the road is not visible, as it is under farm fields. Where the course of the road reaches the old railway, the Romans built a station on a small area of gravel higher than the surrounding marshlands. The road entered the fortified site from the southwest and exited to the northeast toward Pulborough.

The camp was considered to be one day's march from Chichester and provided a safe place to stay for the night. As a military fort, it provided protection for the area and probably a place for local administration and tax collection.

Some remains have been found, but nothing significant. A second Roman road from Lewes cuts through here to meet up at the Roman fort on Stane Street.

Presently at this lovely country scene there is a wedding venue. It looks like a circus tent in a big field, but apparently is an extremely popular spot for wedding receptions.

The old road here goes through what is now a pumping station and industrial site.

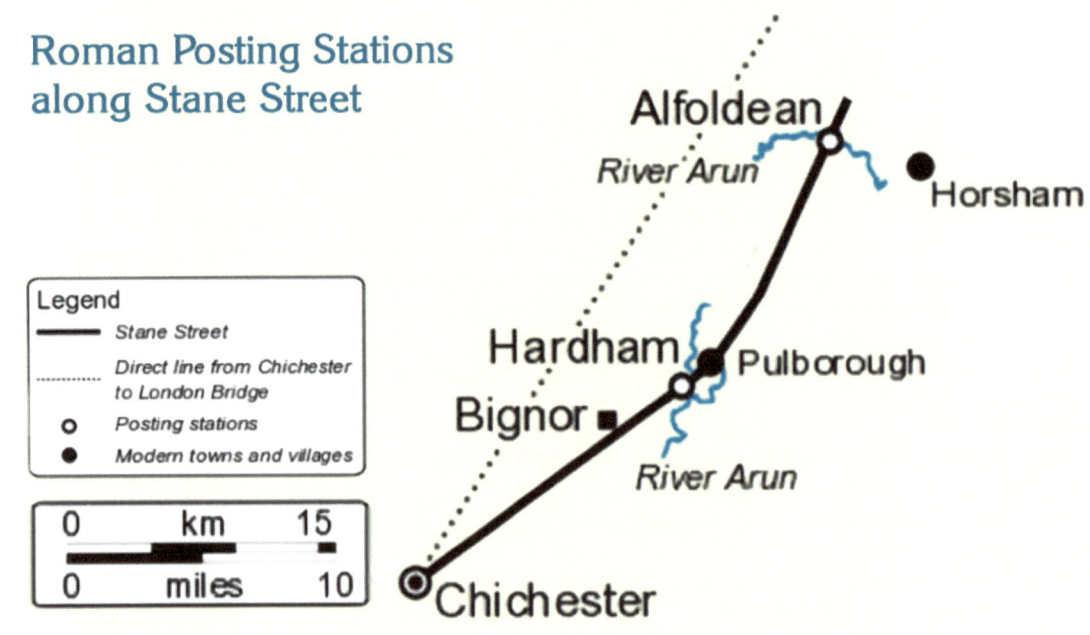

Fig 50: Map of Stane Street

Fig 51: View Across Wetland at Pulborough Brooks

Just to the north, through a water meadow, the public footpath leads over the River Rother and then to the ancient bridge at Stopham.

The bridge was built in 14th century and then rebuilt in the 16th, is only wide enough for one horse and carriage. There are pockets built along the bridge which allowed pedestrians a safe place to stand while wheeled traffic crossed.

The centre space was replaced in 1820 to allow barge traffic to get through.

If we look carefully, we can see the scratch marks on the walls left by tanks during WWII.

On a nice day many locals and tourists sit outside and enjoy a drink and food overlooking river at a lovely old pub on the east side.

Fig 52: Stopham Bridge with the river in spate

Fig 53: Stopham Bridge

A bit farther along is the tiny village of Stopham to the north, with a successful vineyard, a medieval church and some lovely stately homes. Stopham Park is the home of the Barttelot family, which can trace their ancestry back to William the Conqueror.

Pulborough is where the Romans bridged the Arun River. There are records of a small port and a ferry here during medieval times.

A stone bridge was finally built in 1785 at Pulborough near the site of the Roman wooden one.

Pulborough seems to be a town of bridges now, with two originals still standing here over the Arun; the ancient one at Stopham, train bridges, an aqueduct, plus a few footbridges. Archaeological finds show that the town had Roman villas and other buildings including a temple. There are few Saxon remains, but the town did appear in the Domesday book of 1086.

The name comes from old English meaning tidal water and rounded hill. The Arun is tidal here and the church sits on a small hill.

Fig 54: Stopham Bridge

St. Mary's church is built on the site of a Saxon church that was probably built on the site of a Roman temple which overlooked the river. The baptismal font is believed to have come from the Saxon church.

Fig 55: St. Mary's Church Pulborough

Fig 56: *The old Rectory*

St. Mary's has many memorials, on the walls and floors, dating back to the 1400s'.

Pulborough had a particularly busy time during WWII. Many evacuated children from London spent the war here as guests of the townspeople.

In St. Mary's church a painted plaque, from the Peckham schools, dated 1942, is hung for the kindness shown the evacuees during WWII.

At the beginning of the war there were fears that the Germans would invade, landing on the long beaches of Sussex and moving north toward London, which was only 60 miles away.

There was a line of defence called a stop-line where the defenders, mostly Canadian soldiers at this time, would attempt to stop the attacking Germans.

This line ran through Pulborough, as it had the natural defence of the river Arun and was high enough to overlook the plains and downs in front of it.

Many bunkers and defences were built through the area.

Some of these were designed to allow cannon to be rolled in, if and when the time came.

This is one story of a such a bunker, built near Hardham by a private contractor, that faced the wrong way.

If a cannon were to be positioned in it the gun would be facing Pulborough and could shell the town while being completely protected.

The bunker was destroyed by a Canadian Army demolitions crew.

Locals complained about a lot of broken windows.

One sad note is that one of the casualties of the area was the vicar for Hardham and Stopham.

The Rev. William Masefield was ushering a group of school children into a ditch to avoid a German aircraft that was about to strafe them.

He died when struck by a bullet. All the children survived.

His memorial is just south of the Stopham Bridge.

Driving up from the river, one finds two quick roundabouts and then a narrow cut through the ridge.

At the top of the hill there is an old house over the cut on the right, followed by the church on the left and the old rectory, again on the right, which is now an hotel.

In the last century, Pulborough, because of its location having easy access to transportation routes, developed heavy engineering works.

For some reason, this appears to be a good place to look if you are seeking a high-end automobile.

There are a variety of dealerships offering expensive and classic cars.

If you are travelling around here in the autumn try and get to the big, old-fashioned, country harvest fair complete with vintage fairground.

Fig 57: Cow Parsley

Fig 58: Racehorses training

Chapter Five
Pulborough to Slinfold

Following the road north east, we quickly leave the town and descend Codmore Hill back into the country. This is the lowland between the South and North Downs, a very pretty area of farms and villages.

For those interested in horse racing, a racehorse sanctuary is along this stretch of road.

On open days we can visit to learn more or see the old champions.

This part of the road runs very straight with only a couple of interesting stops. There is a good old-fashioned truck stop cafe along here where we can have lunch or a strong tea.

The car can get washed by hand while we are having our meal.

Just beyond this we have to be quick to catch the road sign with the street name 'Gay Street Lane'.

There is a hamlet called Gay Street and this is the lane to get to it; love the names in this country.

Fig 59: Gay Street Lane

Farther along, Stane Street cuts through the middle of Chichester College's Brinsbury Campus. On 570 acres, they specialise in countryside courses including agriculture, forestry and horticulture.

The college has a large herd of cows that supply milk to the local market.

Just past the campus is one of my favourites, a craft beer brewery where we can choose from a large selection of award-winning beers, ales and ciders.

Hepworth has been making high quality craft brews since 2000.

Most of the beers are made with just 4 basic ingredients, organic barley, hops, yeast and water.

They even have a gluten-free ale.

When I cannot decide which to buy, I try their samplers from the lined-up kegs.

Fig 60: Beer Sampler

Two and a half miles north of Pulborough, the road at Todhurst Farm bends 7 degrees north to align with Leith Hill. As Leith Hill is the highest hill in the area, even the Romans knew to avoid it.

Farther along, the route makes a small diversion to pass close to an old coaching inn: The Blacksmiths Arms is now a popular public house and restaurant.

A mile down the road we arrive at the roundabout for the bypass around Billingshurst. This is great, if we are in a hurry, but Billingshurst is a charming village worth seeing. Many traces of Roman activity have been found here. Hurst is a Saxon word for hill and St. Mary's Parish Church has sat on this low hill, overlooking the village, for the last 950 years.

The village was located here because it had water and was surrounded by fertile soil, while most of the surrounding area was clay.

The road did curve around Alick's Hill in order to avoid a steep bank, following the easiest route through the little valley.

The Roman Road made transportation easy before the railway and canal. The road is now a paved carriageway. The railway is on the main run from London's Victoria Station. The canal lost the battle with the railway. Because of its relative quiet and prosperity, the village has many old, fascinating

Fig 61: St. Mary's Church – Billingshurst

buildings. On the high street is a 500-year-old timber framed building.

It started life as a farmhouse but since the 19th century has been a hostelry going now by the name of the Six Bells pub. There are some wonderful walks along the towpath of the partially restored canal.

A couple of miles south east of Billingshurst is the village of Coolham which has a curious part in English and American history. Here we find the Quaker meeting house called the Blue Idol.

This house is another one of those described by Viscountess Francis Wolseley in the 1920's for the Sussex Paper. The name could have been a misspelling of 'idle' as it was vacant for some time and thus idle. The 'blue' comes from the fact that some houses were covered with blue instead of white stucco. It is white now.

Fig 62: Blue Idol

With a shipload of Quakers, William Penn set sail to America in 1682.

There he created what is now the state of Pennsylvania and the city of Philadelphia (the city of brotherly love).

Returning to England in 1691 he was instrumental in purchasing the Blue Idol as a permanent meeting house for local Quakers.

The Quakers here have long been twinned with the group in Philadelphia founded by Penn.

There are meetings here every Sunday.

The building is open at specified times.

Their web site has more detailed information.

Fig 64: Old Cart

Stane Street continues its path north east through Five Oaks where the A264 heads off toward Horsham.

Following straight through it comes close to the country village of Slinfold with its old church along the banks of the Arun River.

There is an old legend concerning a bell that was lost during transport in the marshy bogs near the town.

It could not be found so in desperation the locals turned to a witch who told them that it could be retrieved only at midnight, pulled by twelve white oxen.

There was one more restriction the workmen could not say a word.

When the bell was pulled from the swamp, one of the men cheered at their success.

Having broken the rules, the rope snapped, and the bell rolled back into the bog, never to be found again.

On now to the next Roman fort.

Fig 63: Willam Penn

Fig 65: Slinfold Railway Station 1910

Fig 66: St Peter's parish church, Slinfold

Stane Street: From Chichester to London

Fig 67: Rose Mallow

Fig 68: Roman Garden

Chapter Six
Alfoldean to Ockley

Eleven miles up the road from the Hardam camp, the Romans built another mansio. This time at Alfoldean. This camp too was built on the banks of the Arun River and guarded a bridge. It was considered another day's march from Chichester. This site is huge compared to the one at Hardham.

The mansio provided nice rooms for officials and shared rooms for soldiers and travellers. There was a bath house, courtyards, stables and a dining area.

As this was also an administration area, there was probably a permanent detachment of soldiers plus tax collectors and governors. Over the 250-year period of use it developed a large settlement of locals around the walled and ditched fort. The road ran through the middle of the mansio which had gates at either end and access to the bridge.

Excavations in the 1920s uncovered the encampment measured over 100 metres east/west and 110 north/south. The complete site is over 9 hectares, most of which is under farmers' fields now. The long running Channel 4 TV series Time Team did an episode on this site in 2005, (series 13 episode 12).

The episode is on YouTube if you want more details about his settlement.

There is also a detailed document available on the Wessex Archaeology web site.

After the Romans left in the 3rd century the site fell into disuse. It is easy to miss now, as the only indication on the A29 is a lay-by just south of the bridge. A short walk around the area near the shady banks of the Arun will produce ancient pieces of pottery and building materials.

After crossing the river at Alfoldean, Stane Street runs about 100 metres to the roundabout and the east/west Guildford Road (A281).

The street originally ran up the hill ahead through what is called Roman Woods. It was underused and was eventually abandoned and overgrown. It was easier to go around the hill than over it.

For the next five or six kilometres almost all of it vanishes. Hedgerows and the edges of ploughed fields mark where the road could have been. It passes through the hamlet of Rowhook which in early English means a rough corner of land.

Here another Roman road (Farley Heath road) crosses Stane Street in front of the 15th century inn (now a popular gastro pub).

It then crosses Rowhook Farm and on into more fields, parallels Ruchman's Lane for a bit, comes close to the village of Okewood Hill and rejoins the A29 near the West Sussex/Surrey border.

Okewood Hill also has a 15th century inn turned into a popular gastro pub.

Fig 69: Ockley Village Hall

The 5 km of road through Ockley is built directly on top of the Roman road and has been well used and maintained as there are no hills around or rivers to cross.

Ockley is an enchanting village with a long history and some of the most beautiful houses and buildings that can be found anywhere along the road.

To the west are the cricket grounds and school and to the east is the old village hall. It has one Saxon historic claim to fame. Near here in the year 851, King Ethelwulf (king of Wessex) with his son and a West Saxon army defeated a marauding army of Danes who had just pillaged London. It was said to be a great slaughter.

Reportedly the king and army used Stane Street to march to Ockley.

In 1639 the local rector, Henry Whitfield, along with 25 local families emigrated from here to the New World and founded the town of Guildford in what was to become the American state of Connecticut.

Whitfield's house is one of the oldest in North America. The town itself is considered one of the top 100 best places to live in the US.

Also in Ockley, a windmill, built in 1803, was used until 1912 to grind grain.

It was called Elmer's mill only because it was on Elmer's farm. The Elmer family has lived in the Ockley area since the eleventh century.

The wooden beam over the mill's front lintel had a date inscribed 1532 but that was misleading as it had been salvaged from an old barn near the mill site.

In 1944, after years of dereliction, it finally fell down. Recovered metal was used in the war effort.

Help came in 2005 and, over the next 7 years, the windmill was reconstructed as a private residence.

Please respect the owner's privacy as it is not open to the public but does look lovely on the ridge south of Ockley.

Turning west, just past the Village Hall, the road leads up to Leith Hill Place.

This was opened to the public in 2013 by the National Trust. Originally a residence built around 1600 it was owned by notable families including Wedgwood and Vaughan Williams. It was given to the National Trust in 1944 who leased it out as a boarding house for a nearby school. There are claims that it is haunted (by whom is not certain but odd noises can be heard late at night).

Continue on to the summit of Leith Hill and we find a Gothic tower. It was built by Richard Hull in the 1760s who was the owner of Leith Hill Place at that time.

Fig 70: Leith Hill Place

Fig 71: Leith Hill Tower

It appears that he wanted to raise the hill's summit to 1,000 feet. He encouraged the public to come and visit.

After his death it fell into disuse and was filled with concrete and debris.

In 1864 another local wanted to re-open it but could not get around the concrete.

So he just build a second tower on the outside which connected to the first at the roof.

The view over the downs and hills really is spectacular.

The tower can be seen on the crest of the hill from Stane Street as far back as Alfoldean.

Back on the road we pass Coles Road on our right.

This leads off to the medieval church of St. Margaret with its six bells.

A duplicate of the tenor bell was sent to the city of Philadelphia in 1772 where it cracked. It was recast to fix the crack, but cracked again in the 19th century.

It is now called the Liberty Bell as it was supposedly rung on July 8, 1776 declaring the American independence.

Further on is the lovely, preserved train station which was opened in 1867 and is now a Grade II listed building.

If not for this protection it probably would have been torn down years ago but now Network Rail must maintain it in its present form.

Following the road northeast, again, the A29 makes a 90 degree turn to the right to become the Beare Green Road.

Stane Street itself continues straight for several hundred metres and ends at Buckinghill Farm.

Fig 72: Leith Hill Tower

Fig 73: Ockley Train Station

The farm is described as a timber farm hall house build in the early 15th century with extensions and other buildings built in the 17th and 18th centuries. They sometimes have tours around the medieval farm. Once again, the road disappears under farmer's fields and woodland.

Fig 74: Buckinghill Farm (Cover Picture)

Fig 75: Daisies and Bluebels

Fig 76: Christ Church, Coldharbour, Dorking, Surrey

Chapter Seven
Ockley to Dorking

On the straight line between Buckinghill Farm and Holmwood, the road resurfaces here and there for a little while, before disappearing again at Anstie Lane.

An interesting side trip would be to the north west on this lane. It leads to a "Scheduled Ancient Monument" called Anstiebury Camp.

This a late Iron Age hill fort with much of the earthwork still visible. The best time to explore is in the winter when the leaves are off the trees and many views over the valleys are visible.

It was abandoned as the inhabitants moved to farm lower lands, with Roman protection and civilization.

Just to the south west, the tiny village of Coldharbour is a lovely place to stop for refreshment.

Back on the road, which is now the A24, we find that, according to S.E. Winbolt in his 1930s exploration book, the road turns slightly to the east here to avoid the higher slopes of Leigh hill.

It later turns back north, in more small turns, to continue over the River Mole to Dorking, using the Roman idea of short sections in straight lines.

According to the Dorking Museum, the Romans were the first people to use the 'Mole Gap' to get from the downs and Chichester to London.

After their collapse, no one used this route for centuries. There was a Roman settlement (probably a way station like Harham and Alfoldean) around what is now St. Martin's Church and High Street in Dorking.

Fig 77: Cold Harbour

Dorking, a commuter community roughly 20 miles south of London, has a population of about 11,000. It has been inhabited for thousands of years as Bronze Age tools have been found in the area.

A farming settlement flourished here probably since before Roman times. One of the symbols of the town is the "Dorking Chicken" (reported to have been a favourite of Queen Victoria). It was introduced by the Romans from Italy and is the oldest breed of chicken in Great Britain, set apart because it has five toes and not the usual four.

The town appears in the 1086 Doomsday Book as a holding of William the Conqueror. Later records show the Knights Templar and the Knights of St. John owned property there too.

According to the local museum, in 1649, the local lords created a survey map that shows a town of 1,500 surrounded by a patchwork of farms and small holdings.

The turnpike built in 1750 made Dorking a staging post on the road to Brighton. Some of the original inns are still doing business as pubs in the downtown area.

Fig. 78: Dorking Chicken - Rooster and Hen. Magasin Pittoresque 1880

Fig 79: Dorking, Rainbow over Boxhill

Although many Roman coins have been found around here, little has been found of the station.

Stane Street, itself, has gone, buried under centuries of settlement and what is now modern Dorking.

Today, Dorking is a lively town surrounded by the beautiful Surrey Hills (which offer walking, hiking, cycling and other outdoor activities).

With turnpikes giving quick access, the rich of London were encouraged to buy huge estates and build large mansions around the area. Some of these properties are now owned by the National Trust.

One, Polesden Lacey, was left to the Trust in 1943 by Society Hostess Margaret Greville who, with her husband, had bought it in 1907 as a weekend retreat (on his retirement as the MP for East Bradford).

Sadly, he died in 1908. Remodelling was completed in 1909 by Charles Mewès (1860 – 1914) and Arthur Joseph Davis (1878 – 1951), the architects who designed the Ritz Hotel and the house saw many famous guests.

George VI and Queen Elizabeth spent part of their honeymoon here in 1923 when they were just the Duke and Duchess of York.

The house has been refurbished and now offers the public (free of charge), views of her extensive collection of artwork and walks around the estate. There is a youth hostel in the grounds.

One of the outstanding landmarks of Dorking is St. Martin's parish church with its high clock tower not far from the town centre.

This is a Victorian church, the third built on this site.

Stane Street ran through a corner of the churchyard. Some stones from the road were found when graves were dug in the 19th century.

About one and a half km north of Dorking is a unique crossing of the Mole River.

The 'Stepping stones' were originally put in to replace an old bridge.

During the Second World War they were destroyed as part of anti-invasion measures.

In 1946, seventeen new hexagonal 'Stepping stones' were placed and dedicated to Prime Minister Clement Attlee.

Be careful after heavy rainfall.

The path continues on the North Downs Way and up to the top of National Trust's Box Hill.

The name comes from the grove of Box Trees on the steep west-facing slope of the hill.

The trust maintains walking trails, operates a restaurant and offers family activities throughout the year. There is evidence of Stone Age activity and remains of two Bronze Age barrows.

The property is one of the highest points in the North Downs, overlooking the Mole River and the stunning Surrey Hills.

Also on the west side of Box Hill we find the grave of Peter Labilliere (AKA Labelliere). After a career in the British Army, he became a peace activist.

Fig 80: St Martins

Fig 81: Stepping across the River Mole

Fig 82: Stepping Stones near Dorking

Fig 83: Rainbow over Box Hill and Dorking

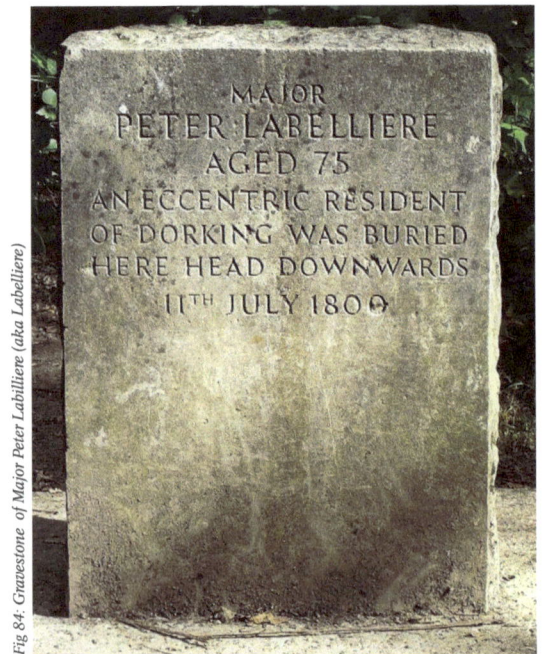

Fig 84: Gravestone of Major Peter Labilliere (aka Labelliere)

He was accused of bribing English troops not to fight in the American War of Independence.

He was so effective that the army had to hire German mercenaries to fight instead.

He retired to Dorking in 1789 and became more eccentric with age. Neglecting his personal hygiene, he was called 'the walking dung hill'.

He loved going to Box Hill to meditate. Labilliere died in June 1800 and his burial was attended by thousands.

Believing the world was 'topsy-turvy' he was buried head down with no religious ceremony.

Fig 85: Elder Blossom

Fig 86: Broadwood's Folly

Chapter Eight
North from Dorking

The A24 continues north from Dorking more or less on the route that Stane Street would have taken.

We cannot know for sure as there are few traces of the road here. Roman coins from the 4th century were found in 1935 near where the road crosses the Southern Railway.

Old records show that there was an 18th century turnpike toll gate just south of the Burford Bridge at the Beehive Public House.

Also, at this point, the Pilgrims Way crosses Stane Street. Since medieval times, this route was used by pilgrims going from Winchester to Canterbury Cathedral where Thomas Becket was murdered.

This route is perhaps the most well-known of British pilgrimages.

At the beginning of the 20th century Hillaire Belloc, who wrote a book about Stane Street, also wrote an excellent book about this old track, called The Old Road.

Since then, as well as pilgrims, many ramblers have walked the North Downs Pilgrims Way.

The 153 miles/245 km of track is maintained by the British Pilgrimage Trust and usually takes about two weeks to walk.

It was also an east-west Roman Road following the North Downs.

Fig. 87: North Downs Way Signpost

Archaeological finds date it to the Bronze Age 500 years before the Romans. Near where the Burford Bridge crosses the River Mole, traces of a Roman bridge were found but are lost now. This cut, through the North Downs between Dorking and Leatherhead, is known as the Mole Gap. Mole is thought to be from the Latin mola, which means mill. Undoubtedly the Romans went this way, as it is the only gap in the North Downs.

Following on from the roundabout passing the hotel, the road now becomes the Old London Road (B2209). We pass the aptly named Zigzag Road on our right, which is the way up Box Hill. Another interesting site we can visit is Broadwoods Folly. Situated on Lodge Hill, slightly north of Box Hill, it is easy to find as it is just off Zigzag Road.

The Folly was built here by Thomas Broadwood, from the piano manufacturing family, who owned Juniper Hall in the early 1800s. There is a sparkling white wine named after it, produced by nearby Denbies Wine Estate.

Beyond this, just before Headley Lane, is the entrance to Juniper Hall. This enchanting country house was built in the 1760s as a public house named The Royal Oak. During one of the extensions being added, two Anglo-Saxon skeletons were found in full battle gear. During WWII the Canadian Army used it for planning the Normandy invasion in 1944.

Fig 88. Juniper Hall

Currently it is owned by the National Trust and since 1947 has been used by the Field Studies Council for studies in science and geography. Stane Street ran through the lawn of Juniper Hall.

From here the road circled Juniper Hill, proceeded straight across Mickleham Downs, then looped around a dip (no sense in not following the contour).

For the next few miles, the street is a public footpath. It passes Mickleham village where in June 1730 a single wicket cricket match was played between Surrey and Sussex. As it was reported in the newspapers of the time, Sussex won.

Also, during WWII a German V2 rocket crashed near the village but luckily did not explode.

Fig 90: Max Aitken, Lord Beaverbrook, 1943

Fig 89: V2 Rocket

For the next mile, the road runs along the edge of Cherkley Court through the Beaverbrook Golf Course at about 30 degree east of north.

Cherkley was built in the 1860s for a wool merchant from Birmingham. In 1910, press baron Lord Beaverbrook bought the estate and lived there for the next 50 years.

Many of the rich and famous of the time stayed as his guest. These included Winston Churchill, H.G. Wells, Harold Macmillan and Rudyard Kipling. The Canadian born newspaper publisher, businessman and politician was highly active during both WWI and WWII.

Since 2010 there has been a legal battle as to the use of the building.

A company wants to turn it into a hotel with a golf course, while the residents want to keep the area undisturbed because of its natural beauty.

Crossing the Reigate Road we can see the Tyrrell's Wood Golf Course on the right.

The old manor house has been beautifully restored and is used as the clubhouse.

We could sharpen our culinary skills at the Surrey Cookery School just 50 metres up the road in the opposite direction.

Crossing the Drive at the club house we continue to the crossroads with Headley Road, where the name Stane Street changes.

The pebbles show through the grass here and is locally known as Pebble Lane.

Walk on and we cross the M25 via a pedestrian overpass.

Fig 91: Tyrrell's Wood Golf House

Fig. 92: M25 Crossing

The Romans would have been impressed with 8 lanes of traffic roaring by at 100 kph.

A little farther on, at a junction with another footpath, is a large stud farm known as 30 Acre Barn.

Fig 93: Thirty Acre Barn Crossing Point

Here the road curves gently to the right and the name changes to Shepherd's Walk.

There are traces of Bronze Age barrows (burial mounds) in this area dating back to 1800 BC.

Not far from here near the village of Ashtead, remains of a Roman villa were found.

Fig 94: Wooded Trail

Also near Ashtead, in July 1943, a brave British pilot brought down his crippled Halifax bomber after a raid on Germany. The crew had all bailed out successfully leaving the pilot and one crew member to crash into an empty field. Both were uninjured but the plane burned.

Stane Street goes straight on through and once more disappears under fields, woodlands and motorways for the next few kilometres.

Following the line toward London we arrive at Woodcote Park. The great house at the park was originally built in 1679.

It passed through the hands of many aristocrats including Charles Calvert, 3rd Baron Baltimore, who was the governor of the US colony of Maryland in the 1680s. It was purchased by the Royal Automobile Club in 1913 as the site of a golf course for its members. During WWI and WWII, it was used by the military as a training facility. The ornate gardens were dug up to grow food. The golf course was a handy landing site for a Hawker Hurricane that was forced to land during the Battle of Britain in 1940.

Onward from here the road heads toward the town of Epsom.

Fig 95: Echinops 'Taplow Blue' Globe Thistle

Fig 96: Epsom Clock Tower

Chapter Nine
Epsom and On to London

At Epsom, in the 17th century, a spring was discovered containing 'Epsom salts'. The salts were originally prepared by boiling off the water from this spring.

Fig 97: Salts and Lavender

Fig 98: Market at the Clocktower, Epsom

Because of the salts, Epsom became a spa town, popular with fashionable people from London and many large houses were built here at that time.

The prominent clock tower in the centre of town where the market is held was built in the 19th century replacing the 17th century watchtower.

Epsom Downs Racecourse is named because of its location in the North Downs. The racecourse coined the word 'derby' which is used for describing horse races at many tracks all over the world.

Fig 99. Keep off the Course (Epsom)

The Derby and the Oaks have been run here since 1789. The Epsom Derby is for thoroughbred 3-year-old racehorses. Popular with the Royal Family, the Queen attends more years than not.

Just beyond Epsom, the road turns slightly northward and through the middle of Ewell near High Street. This was done to avoid the natural springs and associated London Clay, the route keeps to the drier chalk.

Both Epsom and Ewell are on the 'spring line', on the north face of the North Downs. Here the chalk meets the impervious 'London Clay'.

These springs are the start of several rivers. Ewell in old English means spring or river source.

One of the tributaries to the River Thames, the Hogsmill River has its source here. During Roman times there was a large farming community running beside Stane Street, which probably originated in the Iron Age.

The Pre-Raphaelite painters John Millais and William Hunt used scenes from this area as background for some of their paintings. Most notably 'Ophelia' was painted along the Hogsmill River in 1851/52.

Ewell, according to the Domesday Book, was known as Etwelle and held by William the Conqueror. There were 2 mills on the river, even then. One mill, described as the lower mill, had been grinding grain for centuries when in 1730 William Jubb converted it into a paper mill.

After 102 years the new owners converted it back to a grain grinding mill.

There is a local story that highwaymen attempted to steal the profits on their way to London by coach. This was thwarted by the miller's young son who burst into tears and refused to move from his seat which had the cash box underneath it.

Garbrand Hall was built in 1770 by Philip Rowden, a wine merchant from London. The next owner Thomas Barritt built the 'Dog Gate' when expanding the Hall in the late 1795. The dog is a Talbot hound. It has been claimed that the dog's tail was damaged and replaced with a cow's horn.

Fig 100: Dog Gate

Garbrand Hall was replaced in 1969 by the Bourne Hall Meeting Centre. The park is a lovely setting with a lake and gardens in the centre of Ewell.

The old house is gone but the gate remains. Elwell was given over to the Merton Priory in 1158.

At Church Street our Roman road turns east again this time to avoid climbing Epsom Downs.

It goes under the corner of a housing estate and re-emerges as the A24 motorway, named here as one of many 'London Roads'. On the east side is Nonsuch Park, which contains Nonsuch Park House.

Fig 101: Nonsuch Park House

The house shoulld not to be confused with Nonsuch Palace, which was built by Henry VIII. So named as there was supposed to be no palace as great as this anywhere.

It was started in 1538 and required the destruction of the village of Cuddington. Henry VIII showed little real interest in the palace having only visited 3 times. He died in 1547 before the palace was complete. After changing hands many times Charles II gave it to his mistress (Barbara, Countess of Castlemaine) who had it demolished in 1682 and sold the remains as building materials to pay off her gambling debts. Nothing of the once-impressive building remains today. It would have cost more than £100M to build in today's money. English Heritage has declared the palace, gardens and remains of Cuddington Village as a Scheduled Monument.

Fig 102: Ladybird on Cow Parsley

Fig 103: The River Wandle at Morden

Chapter Ten
The Last Twelve Miles

We have just over 12 miles/20km left to reach the original Roman London Bridge.

Everything is now built up and no physical trace of Stane Street remains visible. Occasionally, new construction will turn up bits and pieces without recognising what they are.

The road continues as the A24 to Morden, which is a borough of London with about 50,000 inhabitants.

From 1913 to 1965 the area was called Merton and Morden Urban District.

Morden in old English means large fort or possibly 'town on the moor'.

The road cuts through the St. Lawrence churchyard, the highest point in Morden and down into the town centre where it passes just west of the tube station. This is the last stop on the Northern Line. The line was opened in 1926 and effected the creation of suburbs in what once was peaceful Surrey farmland.

Fig 104: Morden Tube Station

Fig 105: Morden Park Hall Gardens

Continuing, the road passes through Morden Park Hall, which is owned by the National Trust. The Garth family owned the estate for centuries.

The present building was built in the 1770s.

In its time it has been a home, a military hospital, a women and children's hospital, a restaurant and is now a wedding venue.

Our route is now hidden by a mosque and a train yard.

The Baitul Futuh Mosque, finished in 2003 (and redesigned after a massive fire in 2015 damaged its admin block) is the largest mosque in Western Europe.

It is only 700 metres from the Morden tube station.

It can handle 10,000 worshippers at one time and acts as a centre to promote peace and integration between Muslims and Non-Muslims.

No one is sure where the route crosses the River Wandle.

The course of the river has often been changed to facilitate the many mills built along it.

The river was once declared the most polluted river in England due to centuries of heavy manufacturing, mainly textiles.

At one time it powered 68 water wheels.

In recent times with great local effort, the river runs clear, and the brown trout have returned along with various other stocked species.

Fig 106: Water Mill, River Wandle

All remains of Stane Street are long gone beneath industrial sites and housing estates until it passes through the remains of Merton Priory.

The priory was an important centre for religion and education for 400 years. Thomas Becket and Nicholas Breakspeare (Pope Adrian IV) were educated here.

Merton was destroyed in 1538 with the dissolution of the monasteries.

Many of the building stones in Nonsuch Palace came from the Priory. The palace is gone but some of the priory stones remain.

The area became the heart of the British textile industry. The original calico mill, started in the 1752, was purchased by William Morris in 1881 and he used it for dyeing and printing cloth, making stained glass, weaving and making wallpaper. The company was closed in 1940.

In the 1860s a rail line went through here and the Merton Priory Station was built for the workers and deliveries to the many mills built along this part of the Wandle River.

The rail line was closed in 1975 and when they tore down the station they found ruins of the priory. These remain under the A24 which was raised to preserve what was left. There are occasional open days when the ruins can be viewed.

Is it not ironic that the priory was built over a road (Stane Street) and a road was built over the priory?

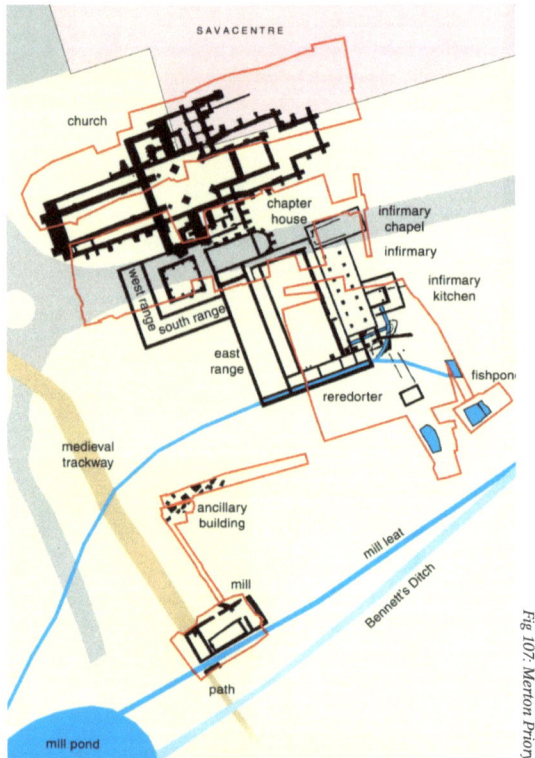

Fig 107: Merton Priory

The A24 swings north-west and then back east to again fall into line with Stane Street at Collier Woods. Just to the west of the high street here, is Wandle Park.

It was once the site of Wandlebank House, built in 1791 by Wandle corn mill owner, James Perry. He was editor of the Morning Chronicle, Georgian London's most popular newspaper.

The house was demolished in 1962.

The park is on the Nelson Trail since Admiral Lord Nelson was thought to have visited the house with Lady Hamilton.

The A24 has been built directly over the priory's charter house.

Fig 108: Wandle Park Croydon - Wandle River

Part is also under the parking lot of the nearby shopping centre. After this it passes through another shopping centre on the High Street, which follows a straight route to Upper Tooting Road.

The name Tooting is said to have been derived from an old English word to tout, to look out. We are told that there could have been a watchtower here on the road to London. The locals were therefore called the people of the look-out post. Following on, Stane Street lines up with Balham High Street over the Balham tube station where in October 1940 during WWII a German bomb exploded in the middle of the road partially destroying the station, killing more than 60 civilians and wounding over 70 more. The bomb created a crater in the middle of the road and a bus fell into the hole.

Fig 109: Bombing Raid

The station had been used as a bomb shelter during the Blitz.

The incident was used in the book and 2007 movie Atonement, when one of the main characters drowns as the water and sewage lines are broken by the bomb.

...Almost there.

Stane Street: From Chichester to London

Fig 110: Cowslip

Fig 111: Kennington Gate Toll Booth c.1865 just outside Kennington Park

Chapter Eleven
The Bridge to Londinium

Along the south-east side of Clapham Common the A24 changes to the A3 and passes Kennington Park on the west side.

The park was originally the Kennington Common.

It was used for public hangings up to 1800 and well known for the cricket matches as early as 1724. In 1898 the 220 acres/89-hectare triangular green space was converted to parkland with duck ponds, bandstand and sporting grounds.

It is surrounded by lovely Georgian and Victorian mansions built by rich Londoners who wanted to get out of the city.

The common has a long rich history of large gatherings with everything from public orators to protest marches to music festivals.

It also has a lovely cafe where we can enjoy a sunny day 'people watching'.

In 1967, the Southwark and Lambeth Archaeological Society excavated a playing field which was sited along the believed route of the old Roman road.

As part of the Henry Thornton School, just off Elms Road in Clapham, the site had never been built on (although the site was riddled with pipes and frequently flooded). Evidence was found that confirmed the existence of an ancient highway that corresponded with the route historically associated with Stane Street.

Fig 112: Kennington Park

Kennington Park Road changes into Newington Butts as it approaches Elephant and Castle. Here the route of Stane Street goes through the large shopping centre. The area got its name from an old coaching inn. The Elephant lodge is mentioned in Shakespeare's Twelfth Night. The area was devastated by bombing during WWII and rebuilt into a major centre with government buildings, residential complexes and the largest covered shopping centre in London. The route is lost again until it lines up at Borough. The area got its name because at the time it was the only borough that London had outside the city. Here the coaching inn called Tabard Inn was the assembly point for pilgrims on their way to Canterbury Cathedral.

Fig 113: Elephant and Castle

It is featured in Chaucer's Canterbury Tales. Nearby St. George the Martyr church is mentioned by Dickens in Little Dorrit.

On to the River Thames to the site of the original Roman bridge, just to the east of the current one. The new one, made of concrete and steel, was opened in 1973 replacing the previous 19th century stone bridge.

Before this was a 600-year-old medieval one, which was a vast improvement on the wooden Roman Bridge built in the 1st century. The original bridge was built to connect the northern area of England to the south. This bridge was protected by a Roman garrison. On the north side, a small trading centre started and was named Londinium. This town soon became the administrative capital of the British Roman Empire. Roads were built to all parts of the empire in a cartwheel pattern.

During Saxon times, the bridge and town fell into disrepair and the river formed the boundary between Wessex and Mercia. For the next few centuries, a timber bridge was built and destroyed a few times depending on who was in power and needed a crossing. The first stone bridge took 33 years to build and was completed in 1209. It was between 800 and 900 feet long supported by 19 arches sitting on the riverbed.

Fig 114: The first Stone London Bridge - Claude de Jongh 1632

For over 350 years, the severed heads of traitors and criminals were displayed on spikes at the south end: William Wallace (Braveheart) was the first in 1305.

By the mid-1350s it had over 100 shops and houses on it with many more to come. The congestion grew so bad that it could take an hour to cross.

The buildings had a tendency to burn once in a while.

Around 1760 all the shops and houses were finally demolished by act of parliament.

The next bridge, opened in 1831, was made of 5 stone arches. By 1900 it was carrying over 8,000 pedestrians and 900 vehicles per hour.

It was widened from 30 feet to 43 feet to accommodate all the traffic.

In 1968 the bridge was sold to an American for $2.4 million.

It was dismantled and shipped to Arizona where it was reassembled over the canal at Lake Havasu.

Rumour has it that the buyer thought he was buying Tower Bridge which is far more impressive.

The current bridge took five years to build and was opened by Queen Elizabeth II in 1973.

This one has only 3 spans but is just as busy as all its predecessors.

Fig 115: Old London Bridge sketch of the demolition March 1832 by William Alfred Delamotte (1775–1863)

Fig 116: London Bridge over Lake Havasu

Fig 117: Current London Bridge from St Olaf's Stairs

Fig 118: The Comet

In the 1830s travellers going to the south coast could take 'The Comet'. It was the latest in transportation at the time. Coaches running to Arundel, Littlehampton and Bognor were the height of luxury. Their route covers much of Stane Street between Leatherhead and Pulborough. By the end of the 19th century the railroads had replaced the horse-drawn coaches and no longer needed Stane Street.

In the last 100 years the automobile has replaced much of the train service and put the road back into use.

That completes the 56 miles from Chichester to London.

For nearly 2,000 years, this road has had many different feet walking or riding on it.

The road is still there in many places with new and different people walking and riding.

I hope this book has put a little life into the scenery and given the reader a sense and appreciation of the people and places that passed before.

Richard Powell

Fig 119: Halnacker Tunnel

Fig 120: Chichester People

List Of Figures & Acknowledgements

1 *Stane Street* - Public Domain - Copyright Expired

2 *Julius Caesar Peter Paul Rubens* - courtesy of the Leiden Collection, NY

3 *Road Construction* - Public Domain - too many variations to source original

4 *Hilaire Belloc c.1903* - Public Domain - Copyright Expired

5 *Bluebells* - © Richard Powell

6 *Chichester Market Cross* - The Mirror Of Literature, Amusement, & Instruction. Vol. XVII. No. 470. 1831

7 *Romans Ancient Times* - Costumes of All Nations (1882) by Albert Kretschmer & Dr. Carl Rohrbach

8 *Chi-rho Motif* - Public Domain - too many adaptations to source original

9 *John Norden 1595 map of Chichester* - John Norden 1595 - Copyright Expired

10 *St Pancras Church* - © Richard Powell

11 *Roman Wall* - © Richard Powell

12 *Litten Park* - © Richard Powell

13 *Spitfire Formation by Gareth Davies Rolls Royce Engines* - © Gareth Davies, York, UK

14 *James Lillywhite 1860s* - Public Domain - Copyright Expired

15 *Goodwood Vintage Auto Race* - Courtesy of Goodwood Estate – Photo © Jochen Van Cauwenberge

16 *Boxgrove Priory and Church* - © Richard Powell

17 *Road up Halnaker Hill* - © Richard Powell

18 *Halnaker Windmill* - © Richard Powell

19 *Vineyard* - © Richard Powell

20 *Wildflowers* - © Richard Powell

21 *Stane Street near Eartham* - © Richard Powell

22 *Great Ballard School* - With thanks to © Great Ballard School

23 *Six Corners* - © Richard Powell

24 *Tree Roots over Stane Street* - © Richard Powell

25 *Gumber Bothy* - © Richard Powell

26 *Stane Street Looking South* - © Richard Powell

27 *Stane Street at Monarch Way* - © Richard Powell

28 *Signpost on top of Bignor Hill* - © Richard Powell

29 *Wealdon Hall* - © Richard Powell

30 *Roman Mosaics* - © Richard Powell

31 *Coke's Hall* - Public Domain – Copyright Expired photo by Charles Drakew

32 *Sign at Bury* - © Richard Powell

33 *Foxglove* - © Richard Powell

34 *St. Giles Church. Coldwaltham* - © Nickos - Nick Hawkes - stock.adobe.com

35 *River Arun* - ©FrontlitPhotography - stock.adobe.com

36 *St. Giles Church. Coldwaltham* - © Nickos - Nick Hawkes - stock.adobe.com

37 *Yew tree at St. Giles* - © Richard Powell

38 *St. Hardham Map* - © www.archiuk.com

39 *Elizabethan House* - © Richard Powell

40 *Frescoes at St. Botoph's* - © Antiquary Creative Commons CC-BY-SA 4.0, Wikimedia Commons

41 *The Wey and Arun Canal* - © paulbriden - Paul Briden stock.adobe.com

42 *Parham House* - © Acabashi, Creative Commons CC-BY-SA 4.0, Wikimedia Commons

43 *The Long Gallery, Parham House* - Edited UPP © Acabashi, Creative Commons CC-BY-SA 4.0, Wikimedia Commons

44 *Parham Gardens* - © Acabashi 2016, Creative Commons CC-BY-SA 4.0, Wikimedia Common

45 *Parham House* - © Acabashi, Creative Commons CC-BY-SA 4.0, Wikimedia Commons

46 *Greatham Bridge Detail* - © Nickos - Nick Hawkes - stock.adobe.com

47 *Greatham Bridge* - © Richard Powell

48 *Morning Glory* - © Garden World Images/Ellen McKnight - stock.adobe.com

49 *The White Hart Public House at Stopham, near Pulborough* - © Nickos - stock.adobe.com

50 *Map of Stane Street* - Edited by UPP © 2010 Mertbiol re-drawn based on I. D. Margary's, 'Roman Ways in the Weald' 1965 edition

51 *View Across Wetland at Pulborough Brooks* - © Alan Whitehead - stock.adobe.com

52 *Stopham Bridge with the river in spate* - © Richard Powell

53 *Stopham Bridge Detail* - © Richard Powell

54 *Stopham Bridge* - © 2014 Oliver Hoffmann - stock.adobe.com

55 *St. Mary's Church Pulborough* - © Richard Powell

56 *The old Rectory* - © Richard Powell

57 *Cow Parsley* - © Richard Powell

58 *Racehorses training* - © frankcornfield.com - stock.adobe.com

59 *Gay Street Lane* - © Richard Powell

60 *Beer Sampler* - © WavebreakmediaMicro - stock.adobe.com

61 *St. Mary's Church – Billingshurst* - © Richard Powell

62 *Blue Idol* - © Richard Powell

63 *Willam Penn* - © Original Copyright Expired Creative Commons CC-BY-SA 4.0, Wikimedia Commons

64 *Old Cart* - © IWeide - stock.adobe.com

65 *Slinford Railway Station 1910* - © Original Copyright Expired (c.1910) Creative Commons CC-BY-SA 4.0, Wikimedia Commons

66 *St Peter's parish church, Slinfold* - © 2011 The Voice of Hassock Creative Commons CC-BY-SA 4.0, Wikimedia Commons

67 *Rose Mallow* - © Richard Powell

68 *Roman Garden* - © antiqueimages - stock.adobe.com

69 *Ockley Village Hall* - © Colin Smith / Village Hall, Ockley / CC BY-SA 2.0

70 *Leith Hill Place* - © Richard Powell

71 *Leith Hill Tower* - © Paul - stock.adobe.com

72 *Leith Hill Tower* - © Marina Marr - stock.adobe.com

73 *Ockley Train Station* - © Andrew Longton Creative Commons CC-BY-SA 4.0, Wikimedia Commons

74 *Buckinghill Farm (Cover Picture)* - © Richard Powell

75 *Daisies and Bluebels* - © Richard Powell

76 *Christ Church, Coldharbour, Dorking, Surrey* - © Bjanka Kadic - Marina Marr - stock.adobe.com

77 *Cold Harbour* - © Richard Powell

78 *Dorking Chicken - Rooster and Hen. Magasin Pittoresque 1880* - ©Morphart - stock.adobe.com

79 *Dorking, Rainbow over Boxhill* - © William Barton - William - stock.adobe.com

80 *St Martins* - © Richard Powell

81 *Stepping across the River Mole* - © William Barton - William - stock.adobe.com

82 *Stepping Stones near Dorking* - © William Barton - William - stock.adobe.com

83 *View from Boxhill* - © Richard Powell

84 *Gravestone of Major Peter Labilliere (aka Labelliere)* - © Poliphilo - Creative Commons CC-BY-SA 4.0, Wikimedia Commons

85 *Elder Blossom* - © Richard Powell

86 *Broadwood's Folly* - © Field Studies Council

87 *North Downs Way Signpost* - © Richard Powell

88 *Juniper Hall* - © Richard Powell

89 *V2 Rocket* - Public Domain - too many adaptations to source original

90 *Max Aitken, Lord Beaverbrook , 1943* - © Yousuf Karsh (1908–2002), Dutch National Archives, (ANEFO), 1945-1989, CC-BY-SA 4.0

91 *Tyrrell's Wood Golf House* - © Richard Powell

92 *M25 Crossing* - © Richard Powell

93 *Thirty Acre Barn Crossing Point* - © Richard Powell

94 *Wooded Trail* (inside Front Cover) - © Richard Powell

95 *Echinops 'Taplow Blue' Globe Thistle* - © Alexandra - stock.adobe.com

96 *Epsom Clock Tower* - © Richard Powell

97 *Salts and Lavender* - © Анна Бортникова - stock.adobe.com

98 *Market at the Clocktower, Epsom* - © Nickos - Nick Hawkes - stock.adobe.com

99 *Keep off the Course (Epsom)* - © teddyh - stock.adobe.com

100 *Dog Gate* - © Richard Powell

101 *Nonsuch Park House* - © Dana - stock.adobe.com

102 *Ladybird on Cow Parsley* ©It4All - stock.adobe.com

103 *The River Wandle at Morden* - © 2015 Abdul Shakoor - stock.adobe.com

104 *Morden Tube Station* - © Sunil060902 - Creative Commons CC-BY-SA 4.0, Wikimedia Commons

105 *Morden Park Hall Gardens* - © 2015 Abdul Shakoor - stock.adobe.com

106 *Water Mill, River Wandle* - © Richard Powell

107 *Merton Priory* - Courtesy of Merton Priory © Illustration: Museum of London Archaeology

108 *Wandle Park Croydon - Wandle River* - © Anthony Spratt - Creative Commons CC-BY-SA 4.0, Wikimedia Commons

109 *Bombing Raid* - © Imperial War Museum - used under the IWM NC Licence

110 *Cowslip* - © Richard Powell

111 *Kennington Gate Toll Booth c.1865 just outside Kennington Park* - Edited by UPP © Archivist - Copyright Mary Evans Picture Library 2017 - stock.adobe.com

112 *Kennington Park* - © BasPhoto - stock.adobe.com

113 *Elephant and Castle* - © Presiyan Panayotov - stock.adobe.com

114 *The first Stone London Bridge - Claude de Jongh 1632* - © Yale Center for British Art - Creative Commons CC-BY-SA 4.0, Wikimedia Commons

115 *Old London Bridge - sketch of the demolition March 1832 by William Alfred Delamotte (1775–1863)* - © Abbott and Holder - Creative Commons CC-BY-SA 4.0, Wikimedia Commons

116 *London Bridge over Lake Havasu* - © Jörg Hackemann - stock.adobe.com

117 *Current London Bridge from St Olaf's Stairs* - © Jordiferrer - Creative Commons CC-BY-SA 4.0, Wikimedia Commons

118 *The Comet* - 1903 Copyright expired - from "Stage-Coach And Mail In Days Of Yore" Vol. I Charles G. Harper

119 *Halnacker Tunnel* - © 2020 Julian Gazzard - stock.adobe.com

120 *Chichester People* - Edited by UPP © JwlOwen - stock.adobe.com and © Javier Cuadrado - stock.adobe.com

www.ingramcontent.com/pod-product-compliance
Lightning Source LLC
Chambersburg PA
CBHW040057160426
43192CB00002B/99